Gran Remembers

by Mio Debnam
illustrated by Isabel Muñoz

Gran took out a box. There were cards, maps and prints inside.

"Oh, look at these," Gran smiled.
"They show me when I was little."

"Cool!" said Jin. "Please can you tell me again about growing up in Japan?"

“This is me in my hometown,” said Gran.
“It is next to the sea.”

"Like this?" asked Jin.

"Yes, but it's cool in December. And hot in June!" said Gran.

“It was a big place, even then,” said Gran. “Lots of roads, shops and homes.”

"This was our landmark," Gran said.

"Was it the home of a ruler?" asked Jin.

“No,” said Gran. “But it was home to many people of power.”

Gran looked at the print again. “I liked this park.”

“I rode my bike under the trees. They had many pink flowers,” she said.

Jin picked a new print from the pile.
"Is this you?" he asked.

Gran's face lit up. "Yes! It was to celebrate New Year," she said.

"I love the New Year broth," said Jin. "Those rice cakes are so good!"

"I love them too!" said Gran with a sigh. She looked sad.

Jin gave her a big hug. “Do you miss Japan?” he asked.

“Sometimes,” said Gran. “This place was hard at first. I could not understand anyone.”

“I was sad and so confused. I just wanted to hide,” Gran said.

"Grandpa hoped I would perk up," Gran said. "He said it would get better."

"Did it?" asked Jin.

"Yes!" said Gran. "Now I love my home in this place."

"But we will all visit Japan soon,"
Gran smiled.

"I am excited to go," said Jin. "I want to see the places we spoke about!"

"I am so pleased," said Gran. "Soon I will visit Japan again!"

Look Back

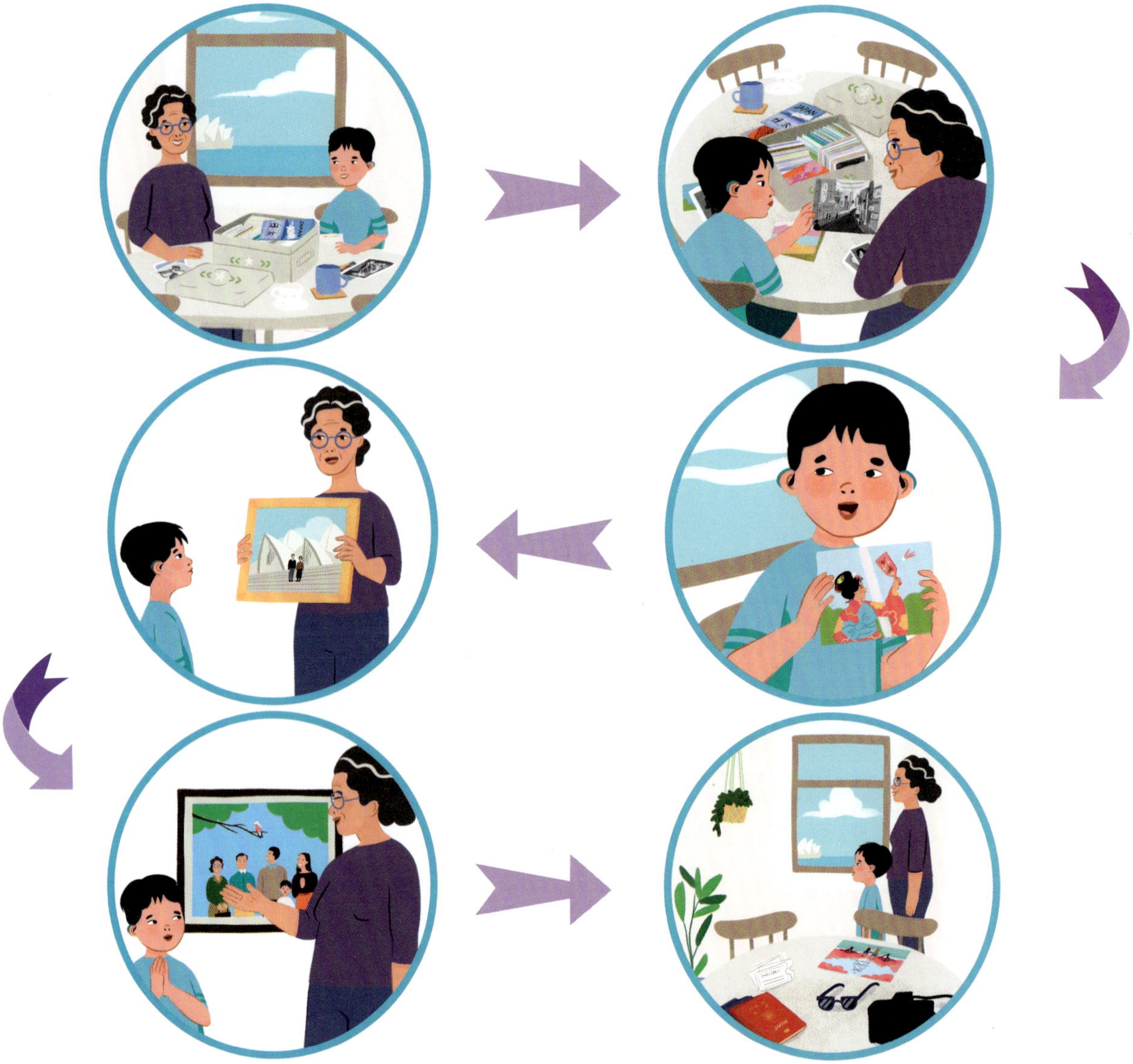

Encourage students to use the pictures to retell the story.